WHAT IT TAKES TO BE A PRO
FOOTBALL PLAYER

by Joanne Mattern

STORY LIBRARY

MORE TO EXPLORE

www.12StoryLibrary.com

12-Story Library is an imprint of Bookstaves.

Photographs ©: Peter B Joneleit/Associated Press, cover, 1; Jeff Thrower/Shutterstock.com, 4; Richard Paul Kane/Shutterstock.com, 5; Arthur Eugene Preston/Shutterstock.com, 6; Arthur Eugene Preston/Shutterstock.com, 7; PD, 8; PD, 9; John Panella/Shutterstock.com, 10; Glen Jones/Shutterstock.com, 11; rick seeney/Shutterstock.com, 12; fayjo/CC2.0, 13; Marianne O'Leary/CC2.0, 14; Associated Press, 15; Henrik Lehnerer/Shutterstock.com, 16; Clemed/CC3.0, 17; RD_Production/Shutterstock.com, 17; Debby Wong/Shutterstock.com, 18; Aspen Photo/Shutterstock.com, 19; Jerry Sharp/Shutterstock.com, 20; Chris Williams/Icon Sportswire 007/Newscom, 21; Coemgenus/CC3.0, 22; Erik Drost/CC2.0, 23; Steve Broer/Shutterstock.com, 24; Allen Eyestone/ZUMA Press Inc/Alamy, 25; Astanhope/PD, 26; michelmond/Shutterstock.com, 27; Jeffrey Beall/CC3.0, 27; Jeff Olivier/Shutterstock.com, 28; Underwood & Underwood/PD, 29

ISBN
9781632357618 (hardcover)
9781632358707 (paperback)
9781645820444 (ebook)

Library of Congress Control Number: 2019938637

Printed in the United States of America
July 2019

About the Cover

San Diego running back Terrell Watson (39) rushes against the Atlanta Legends in 2019.

Access free, up-to-date content on this topic plus a full digital version of this book. Scan the QR code on page 31 or use your school's login at 12StoryLibrary.com.

Table of Contents

Life as a Football Pro: The Real Story

Running, kicking, throwing, catching. There's always a lot of action on the football field. Maybe you want to be part of the action. Life would certainly be exciting if you were an NFL player.

Of course, playing football and getting paid for it is a great dream. But very few people ever live that dream. And living that dream is a lot of hard work.

It is almost impossible to make it to the NFL. There are more than 1 million high school football players. Each year, the NFL has about 300 openings.

Many NFL players are in pain all the time. They often play when they are hurt. Alex Mack played center for the Atlanta Falcons. In 2017, he broke a bone in his leg two weeks before the Super Bowl. There was no way he could play in the big game, right? Wrong! Mack started the game despite his injury.

Most NFL players only play for a few years. Still, when asked if they would do it all again, 89 percent of retired NFL players said yes.

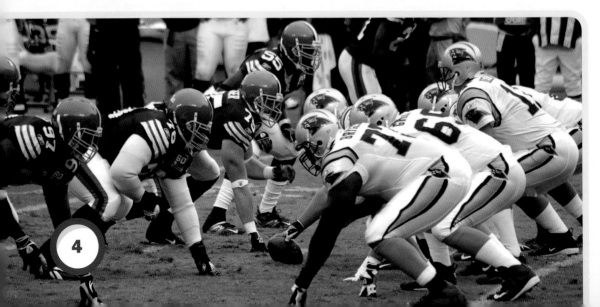

Many pro football players play despite their injuries.

$840,000
Median annual salary for all NFL players

- Superstars make way more. Quarterback Peyton Manning earned $250 million in salary over his NFL career.
- Professional baseball, basketball, and hockey players all make more money per year than NFL players.
- Except for big stars, if a player is injured or cut from the team, he is not paid for the rest of his contract.

WHAT ABOUT GIRLS?

While some girls play with boys on high school football teams, they are almost always kickers. These girls don't get a shot at the NFL. While there are some women's football leagues, such as the Women's Football Alliance (WFA), none pays enough for its players to earn a living.

A Day in the Life

Practice starts early for professional football players.

A pro football player's day starts as early as 6:30 a.m. Players eat a big breakfast. They might eat as often as four times a day. But they also have to stay in shape. Players have weight limits. Offensive guard Tim Lelito reported that his team fined him $550 for every pound he went over his limit. If he gained three pounds, that was a $1,650 fine.

Practice starts around 8 a.m. Players meet with coaches. They talk about different strategies and game plans.

Then they go out on the field. They run drills and train for several hours.

On game days, players arrive at least two hours before kickoff. They meet with the trainer and get taped up for the game. Some receive medical treatments. After they get dressed, some players go back on the field for a light workout. Others prepare by listening to music. Some players like to sit quietly and think about the game. Finally, the team gathers to say a short prayer together. Then they run through the tunnel and start the game.

After the game, players might talk to the media or to players on the other team. Then it's time to peel off that sweaty uniform and take a shower. Another game day is over.

Players need to stay in shape to avoid being fined.

1
Days off per week players get during the season

- The regular season lasts about four months, from September to January. Tuesday is their day off.
- Each team plays 16 games per season.
- In early February, the winning teams from the American Football Conference (AFC) and the National Football Conference (NFC) meet in the Super Bowl.

A Brief History of the Game

Football traces its beginnings to rugby and soccer. After the Civil War (1861–1865), football clubs were popular in many cities around the nation. The game soon spread to colleges. On November 6, 1869, teams from two New Jersey universities, Princeton and Rutgers, played the first college football game.

In those days, football was still a lot like rugby. Then a man named Walter Camp helped start the Intercollegiate Football Association. The IFA changed many of the rules. It introduced the 11-man team. It also introduced the down system. In football, a down is a play. The offensive team has four downs to move the ball 10 yards. If the team succeeds, it gets another four downs. If it doesn't, the other team gets the ball.

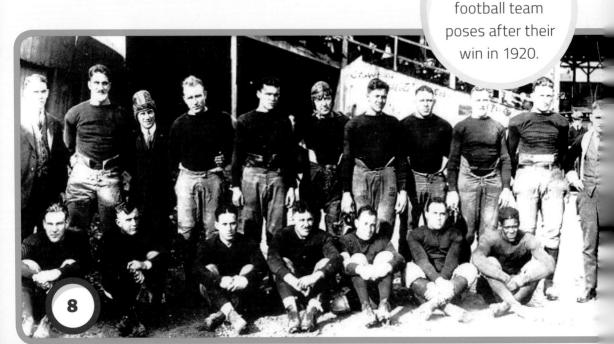

The Akron Pros football team poses after their win in 1920.

$500

How much football's first pro was paid to play a game

- On November 12, 1892, William "Pudge" Heffelfinger played in a game between the Allegheny Athletic Association and the Pittsburgh Athletic Club
- Heffelfinger's team, the AAA, won.
- The document listing Heffelfinger's payment is called "pro football's birth certificate."

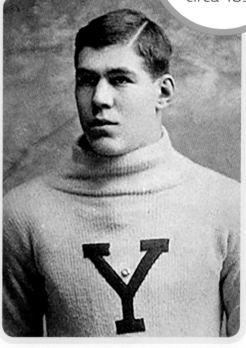

William "Pudge" Heffelfinger circa 1891.

The American Professional Football League formed in 1920. Two years later, it changed its name to the National Football League. Another league called the American Football League formed in 1929. Both leagues played separately until 1970. Then they combined into the National Football League. The NFL has two conferences based on the original leagues. They are the American Football Conference (AFC) and the National Football Conference (NFC). Each conference has 16 teams.

Today the NFL is America's most popular sport. College football is in third place, behind major league baseball. Millions of people play and watch football, cheering on their favorite teams and players.

Clubs and Schools

Some NFL pros started young. Quarterback Peyton Manning, safety Earl Thomas, and linebacker Clay Matthews all played Pop Warner football when they were kids. Pop Warner is the largest youth football organization in the United States. But other pros started late. Defensive end Jason Pierre-Paul didn't play football until he got to college. Tight end Antonio Gates didn't play until after college.

Many adults worry that tackle football is too rough for young children. Kids who play in leagues can be hit in the head hundreds of times each season. This can lead to brain problems later in life. Today more young children play flag football

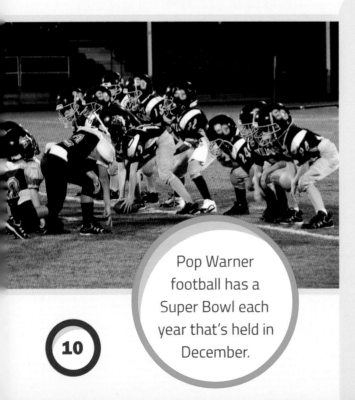

Pop Warner football has a Super Bowl each year that's held in December.

6.57 million

Number of young people in the United States who played flag football in 2018

- In 2006, 8.4 million young people played tackle football.
- By 2018, that number had fallen to 5.22 million.
- Flag football is becoming more popular.

than tackle football. In flag football, there is no body contact.

Older boys and girls can play on middle school and high school football teams. These teams are great ways to learn skills and compete against others. The best high school players are recruited by colleges. They often receive large scholarships. Playing in college is the best way to move on to the NFL.

Many young men and women also enjoy flag football. The NFL's Flag Football League is the largest in the nation. Boys and girls ages 5 to 17 can play year-round.

SUMMER TRAINING CAMPS

Summer training camps are very popular with high school football players who are serious about the sport. These camps are usually held at local high schools or colleges. Players are taught by experienced coaches. Some camps even have former NFL players and coaches on staff. Young athletes can improve their skills and stay in shape before school and football season start in the fall.

Going to College

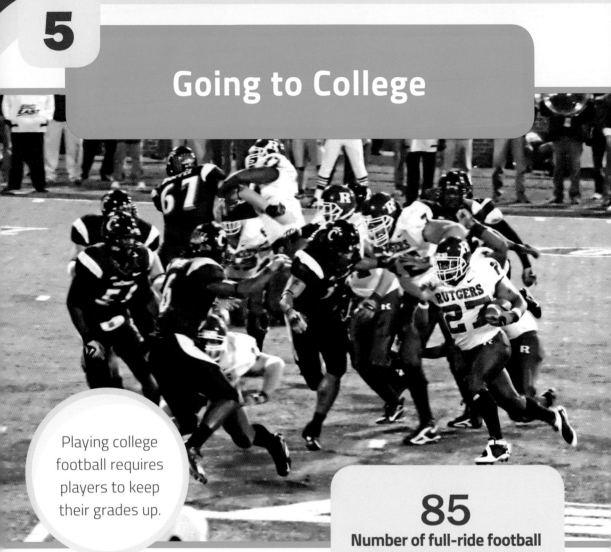

Playing college football requires players to keep their grades up.

The NFL does not take players right out of high school. Pro football, unlike other sports, does not have a minor league system. The best chance for most players to join the NFL is from college.

Playing football at a top college can be a great experience. Players bond with their teammates.

85

Number of full-ride football scholarships available for each Division I school

- There are about 130 Division 1 football teams.
- Division II teams can give out 36 scholarships.
- The odds of getting a full-ride scholarship to a Division I school are less than 1 in 100.

They spend most of their time playing football. Myles Jackson was a defensive end at Rutgers University. He once said that playing football in college is the greatest thing in the world.

It is also hard work. Jackson reported that players must follow a strict schedule. They give up vacations and holidays. There is also a lot of academic pressure. Even though playing football is like having a full-time job, a player can be kicked off the team if he doesn't keep his grades up.

NFL scouts keep an eye on college players. They go to games. They review videos sent by coaches and players.

THREE DIVISIONS

College athletics are divided into three divisions. The top schools are in Division I. Athletics is the focus at these schools. Division II schools put more of a focus on balancing athletics and academics. Division III schools do not make athletics their main focus. They are not allowed to give out athletic scholarships.

Scouts collect data and study it to pick the top players. They want to find players who can make it in the NFL.

Draft Day

Draft day is probably the biggest day in a football player's college career. This is the day that can make a player's dream come true or end his football journey.

The NFL Draft is held in late April. Each of the 32 NFL teams receives a pick in each of the seven rounds of the draft. The team with the worst record gets the first pick in each round. There is a time limit for each pick. The draft lasts for three days. That's how long it takes for the 256 players to be chosen.

Top college players are usually the first picks. However, not all future NFL stars were tops in the draft. Legendary players like quarterbacks Bart Starr and Tom Brady were picked in later rounds.

First-round picks are invited to attend the draft. They usually sit in a room

1936

Year when the first NFL Draft was held

- The idea for the draft came from Philadelphia Eagles owner Bert Bell.
- Bell was tired of owning a losing team and seeing the top teams get the best players.
- Six No. 1 draft picks have led their teams to the Super Bowl.

MORE WAYS TO MAKE THE TEAM

Not every college player is picked in the NFL draft. Those who aren't picked become free agents. They can sign with any team that wants them. The NFL also holds showcases called "combines" to find players. Anyone can pay a fee to attend these events.

and wait for their names to be called. Other picks wait for a phone call at home.

Being picked in the draft is an exciting experience. Top picks become media stars. However, Troy Vincent, a first-round pick in the 1992 draft, reminds players to stay humble. Draft day is just the start of a long and uncertain journey.

Bert Bell with his Philadelphia Eagles in 1939.

Staying in Top Shape

NFL athletes must be at the top of their game. To stay in shape, players train constantly and train hard. NFL workouts focus on power, strength, and speed. An athlete lifts different kinds of weights to strengthen his arms, legs, and core. He jumps rope and runs. Each exercise is repeated dozens or even hundreds of times.

NFL athletes also cross-train. Quarterback Russell Wilson adds boxing to his off-season workouts. Wide receiver Odell Beckham Jr. and linebacker Von Miller

do drills with tennis balls to improve their agility and speed. Many pro players have amazing upper body routines. These can include flipping huge tires or pulling heavy sleds.

Players must also be mentally tough. It's not enough to be competitive and want to win. The best players also need to be patient. They need to be able to see the game as a big picture and not get caught up in the moment. They can't let their emotions get the better of them or be distracted by anything besides

1,000

Weight in pounds (454 kg) of a tire flipped by defensive end J.J. Watt during workouts

- Watt can lift over 700 pounds (318 kg).
- He is six feet, five inches (1.95 m) tall and weighs almost 300 pounds (136 kg).
- He eats between 6,000 and 9,000 calories a day.

THINK ABOUT IT

Besides working out, how can a football player stay physically and mentally tough?

Tim Tebow warming up before a game.

the game. And they have to believe in themselves.

In high school, Tim Tebow was told he would never play college football as a quarterback. In college, people said he would never go pro. He did both. The best players are a combination of mental and physical toughness.

17

Taking a Risk

All that running and smashing into each other can be very hard on a player's body. Football players suffer from many different injuries. Some are minor. Others can end a career or change a person's life forever.

Knee injuries, such as torn ligaments, have been the most common problem since 2000. Kickers often injure the tendon that connects the kneecap to the bones in the leg. Foot and ankle sprains and pulled tendons happen when players change direction at high speeds. Spinal injuries occur when a tackle goes wrong.

Since NFL games are played on live TV, viewers sometimes see horrible injuries happen. In 1985, quarterback Joe Thiesmann suffered a broken leg when he was tackled by linebacker Lawrence Taylor. The injury ended his career. Thirty-three years later to the day, quarterback Alex Smith broke his ankle after being sacked. Once again, TV viewers saw the moment up close on their screens.

The NFL monitors training to make sure athletes play safe. They also make sure their equipment offers the best protection. Sometimes game rules are changed to make play safer.

Helmet-to-helmet hits can cause concussions.

POST-CONCUSSION SYNDROME

Concussions are common in football. Doctors noticed that many former NFL players had a serious brain disease called post-concussion syndrome. All those hits to the head had permanently damaged their brains. Today athletes, coaches, and trainers are more careful about concussions. The NFL has also banned helmet-to-helmet hits in an effort to lower the number of brain injuries.

214
Number of concussions reported in the NFL in 2018

- This number was the lowest since 2014.
- 161 concussions happened during games.
- 53 concussions happened during practices.

Putting on the Gear

Because football is such a violent game, the gear players wear is important. The helmet is probably a football player's most important piece of gear. A helmet protects the player from head and brain injuries. It is made of a hard plastic shell. The inside of the helmet is padded. It may also include air pockets to cushion the head. Helmets have a face mask to protect the player's face. Face masks also prevent an opponent from grabbing a player's face or neck. Players wear mouth guards to protect their teeth and tongue.

Pads cushion the player's body from hits and damage from falling or being knocked down. A player wears pads on his shoulders, thighs, and knees. Some pads also cover the elbows and the tops of a player's arms.

Football players need protection from head to toe.

The soles of football shoes are covered with sharp cleats. These prevent players from slipping on the ground as they run. Cleats come in

WEARING THE HELMET

Football players were not always required to wear helmets. Historians believe the first helmet was worn by a player in 1893. Players wore leather helmets until the 1930s, but there was no rule saying they had to. It wasn't until 1939 that college football required helmets. The NFL didn't require helmets until 1943.

99
Numbers worn by NFL players

- Different positions wear different numbers from 1 to 99.
- Quarterbacks wear numbers 1 to 19. So do kickers. Offensive linemen wear 50 to 79.
- NFL jersey numbers are eight inches high and four inches wide.

different lengths. The size a player wears depends on his position, the conditions on the field, and whether the field is made of grass or artificial turf.

The Vicis Zero1 helmet is designed to soften blows to the head.

UNIVERSITY of WASHINGTON VICIS

LODE SHELL™

CORE LAYER™

ARCH SHELL™

FORM LINER™

10

The Pro Football Hall of Fame

The Pro Football Hall of Fame opened in Canton, Ohio, in 1963. Canton was chosen because that's where the American Professional Football Association (later the NFL) was founded. Another reason was the Canton Bulldogs were a powerhouse team before the NFL was formed. They were also the NFL's first two-time champions.

Every Hall of Famer has a bronze bust in the museum. Visitors can see the busts and use interactive features to learn more about each individual. There is also a special gallery focused on the Super Bowl. Other exhibits feature famous moments and people in the sport, as well as celebrations of football's importance in American life.

Potential Hall of Famers are nominated by fans. Any fan can nominate any player. A fan can also nominate a coach or another person

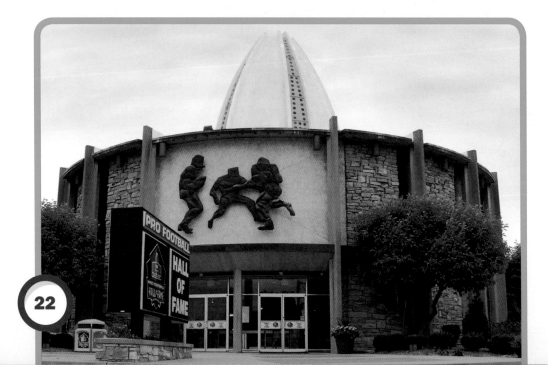

Every Hall of Famer has a bronze bust.

326
Hall of Fame members as of 2019

- The Class of 1963 included legendary athlete Jim Thorpe.
- The smallest classes were 1973 and 1976, when only three people were inducted each year.
- The Chicago Bears have 33 Hall of Famers, the most of any team.

who has contributed to the game in other ways. Players or coaches must have been retired for at least five years to be nominated.

Players are chosen for the Hall by a selection committee. The committee has 48 members. Most are members of the media. Two are Hall of Famers. Through a series of votes, the committee narrows down the list and votes yes or on the finalists. The newest Hall of Famers are named on the night before the Super Bowl. Between four and eight new members are enshrined each year.

Along with a bronze bust, new Hall of Famers get a gold jacket. They also receive the Hall of Fame Ring of Excellence.

After the Game

Professional football players make good money while they play. However, their careers are usually short. The NFL Players Union says the average career lasts just three and a half years. Many players joke that "NFL" actually stands for "Not for Long."

What do NFL players do after they retire? Some go into broadcasting. ESPN and other sports networks often use recently retired NFL players because they know so much about the game. Other retired players find jobs as coaches.

Many go to work for medical companies. NFL players suffer so many injuries that they learn a lot about medical equipment and treatments. Stryker, a company that makes replacement joints and other medical equipment, is the top employer of former NFL players.

Other players struggle to find a life after football. For many, playing in the NFL is the most exciting time of their lives. It happens when they're in their twenties. Then it's over. What next? Former quarterback Trent Green says it is hard to start

Chris Colinsworth (right) went into sports broadcasting after playing with the Cincinnati Bengals.

THINK ABOUT IT

What are some of the pros and cons of being famous and successful when you're young?

68,000
Number of miles (109,435 km) on the car tackle Roman Oben drove when he played for the New York Giants

- Oben was teased for his frugal ways.
- Many players retire without enough money to live on.
- Oben says the key to success is self-worth, not net worth.

Former NFL player and Rhodes Scholar, Myron Rolle, shares his athletic and academic success story.

a new routine after following pro football's strict schedule of workouts and games. Former running back Tiki Barber spent 18 straight months watching TV.

It can take three to five years for a retired player to figure out what he wants to do for the rest of his life. The NFL has programs that can help retired players transition into successful lives after football.

Doing Good and Giving Back

Football players may seem rough and tough, but many have hearts of gold. Individual players and the NFL have raised millions of dollars for charity.

Tom Brady rides to raise funds for Best Buddies International.

Superstar quarterback Tom Brady devotes a lot of time to Best Buddies International, which helps people with disabilities. Between 2011 and 2017, he raised more than $20 million for the nonprofit organization. Brady missed the beginning of the 2018 NFL training season because he was out of the country working for Best Buddies.

Chris Long was a defensive end for several NFL teams. He retired in 2019 but stayed active with his charity, the Chris Long Foundation. The foundation creates opportunities and supports education for young people. In 2017, Long donated his entire salary to fund scholarships in his hometown in Virginia.

J.J. Watt is a defensive end for the Houston Texans. In 2017, Houston was struck by Hurricane Harvey. Watt saw the terrible damage and wanted to help. He pledged to raise $200,000 for hurricane relief. He

$180,971

Amount donated to the Salvation Army after a stunt by Dallas Cowboys running back Ezekiel Elliott

- In December 2016, Elliott jumped into a giant Salvation Army kettle at AT&T Stadium after rushing for a touchdown.
- In the next 24 hours, donations to the Salvation Army poured in. Many were multiples of 21, Elliott's number.
- Elliott donated $21,000.

ended up raising $41.6 million. Watt says that since people follow sports stars, athletes should use that attention to make the world a better place.

THINK ABOUT IT

Is it important for professional athletes to be active in community and charity events? Give reasons for your answer.

J.J. Watt, defensive end for the Houston Texans, used his NFL status to raise over $41 miilion dollars for Hurricane Harvey relief.

Fun Facts about Football

- The first televised football game took place in 1939. Only 500 people watched it.

- The NFL plays almost every game on a Monday, Thursday, or Sunday.

- Since 1941, the Wilson Sporting Goods Company has made all the footballs used in the NFL. The company makes 4,000 balls a day.

- On November 28, 1929, fullback Ernie Nevers scored 40 points in a single game. He scored six touchdowns and four extra points. His feat is the oldest record in the history of the NFL.

- On December 8, 2013, placekicker Matt Prater scored a 64-yard field goal. So far, it is the longest kick in NFL history. Only 20 field goals of 60 yards or more have been made in NFL regular season games.

- The huddle was first used in 1890. Quarterback Paul Hubbard was deaf. He thought the other team was stealing his hand signals, so he had his players stand around him in a circle.

- A football field is marked with lines so players know how far they have to go to score a down.

- In the past, touchdowns were only worth four points. Field goals were worth five points. Today touchdowns are worth six points and field goals are worth three.

- College footballs have white stripes painted on either end. The stripes make it easier to see the ball in the air.

- The last scoreless NFL game was in 1943, when the Detroit Lions and the New York Giants ended with a 0–0 tie.

- The Miami Dolphins are the only NFL team to have an undefeated season. They won every game in 1972. They also won the Super Bowl.

- Defensive back Deion Sanders played both professional football and baseball. He is the only player to score a touchdown and a home run in the same week. Sanders is also the only person to play in both the Super Bowl and the World Series.

Ernie Nevers holds the oldest record in NFL history for scoring 40 points in a single game.

Glossary

academic
Having to do with education.

agility
The ability to move quickly and easily.

concussion
A traumatic brain injury caused by a blow to the head.

conferences
Organizations of sports teams that play each other.

draft
A procedure where teams select new players.

enshrine
To add to and keep in a place that is highly respected and admired.

foundation
An organization that gives money to charity.

frugal
Careful with money.

full ride
A scholarship that covers all the costs of college.

leagues
Groups of sports clubs.

nominate
To propose someone to receive an award.

recruit
To ask someone to join a team or organization.

scholarship
Money paid to support a student's education.

scouts
People who look for talented players to add to a team.

strategies
Plans of action to achieve something.

Read More

Frederick, Shane. *Pro Football Records: A Guide for Every Fan.* North Mankato, MN: Compass Point Books, 2019.

Fuchs, Jeremy. *The Greatest Football Teams of All Time.* New York: Liberty Street, 2018.

Lyon, Drew. *Football's Best and Worst: A Guide to the Game's Good, Bad, and Ugly.* North Mankato, MN: Capstone Press, 2018.

Nagelhout, Ryan. *Becoming a Pro Football Player.* New York: Gareth Stevens, 2015.

Visit 12StoryLibrary.com

Scan the code or use your school's login at **12StoryLibrary.com** for recent updates about this topic and a full digital version of this book. Enjoy free access to:

- Digital ebook
- Breaking news updates
- Live content feeds
- Videos, interactive maps, and graphics
- Additional web resources

Note to educators: Visit 12StoryLibrary.com/register to sign up for free premium website access. Enjoy live content plus a full digital version of every 12-Story Library book you own for every student at your school.

Index

About the Author

Joanne Mattern has been writing books for children for more than 25 years. She loves to write about sports and thinks football is pretty cool. Joanne lives in New York State with her family.